Night Sea Journey
The Ordeal of Individuation

A True Story

James V. Downton, Jr., Ph.D.

Contents

Dedication

This account of my personal transformation is for those who are curious to learn about individuation as a Night Sea Journey and, most importantly, for those who are making their way in that difficult inner terrain; to help them find their way, to let them know that they are not alone, and to give them assurances about the outcome. Involved in a natural process of change known around the world for hundreds of years, these are the people who have entered uncharted territory as pioneers seeking to transform human consciousness.

Introduction

Unbelievable as it might seem, there is a hidden potential to experience a dramatic transformation of consciousness within each of us. Some people refer to this profound and disturbing change as a journey, others as an ordeal. It is both and it goes by different names: "The Night Sea Journey," "Individuation," "Kundalini Awakening," the "Heroic Quest," and "Spiritual Emergency." Its names are many because the human mind cannot fully understand what causes sweeping changes of consciousness.

This book reveals the many trials I faced and the healing that arose from my transformation ordeal. I hope that sharing my story will deepen our understanding of Carl G. Jung's ideas about "individuation," which is the process of achieving psychological integration and wholeness.

My certainty about this dramatic form of transformation arises, not because I understand anything about the Truth, but because a person who has gone through the experience can speak with confidence about it; just as one who takes a trail to a mountain lake is certain about what happened, what was seen, its difficulty, and the surrounding terrain. In this light, I've been over the challenging inner terrain of this overpowering change. However, I remain in doubt about the larger issues of what drives the transformation process, how it can lead to wholeness, and its ultimate meaning in a life which must inevitably end in death. I am content to live in that doubt and to enjoy the mystery of what I cannot understand.

1

The Night Sea Journey

On May 11, 1980, forces from the unconsciousness came like a flood to overwhelm me. This flood was accompanied by a burning heat. It was the dramatic beginning of my Night Sea Journey and it lasted for seven years. It was the most frightening, difficult, and lonely experience of my life. There were moments when it felt like a life and death struggle, but eventually it turned into a blessing because it healed me at a deep level. I learned that my experience was similar, but not as powerful or devastating as Gopi Krishna's ordeal, which he describes in *Kundalini: The Evolutionary Energy in Man*. Like him, I was heated, torn apart, and put back together in a new way.

After the culmination of my change in 1987, I discovered that Carl Jung was keenly aware of the more powerful form that personal transformation can take, which was why he drew on alchemy to reveal the underlying dynamics of individuation, the process of becoming a more integrated person. I learned that the alchemists knew about the great difficulties and dangers of this spontaneous and disturbing experience of white heat and personal crisis. They also understood its great healing power which they attributed to the successful union of opposites and the creation of the "Philosopher's Stone."

I came across the myth of the Night Sea Journey after my change reached its culmination in 1987. It is an ancient myth found in different parts of the world with slight variations. The following version is Leo Frobenius', who constructed a unified myth from many versions.[1] It is a story about a hero who is devoured by a water monster in the West which travels toward the East. This movement suggests the passage of time as a sea journey, but going east is also the goal. During this journey, the hero lights a fire in the belly of the monster. Due to the great heat of the fire, he loses all of his hair. Feeling hungry, he cuts and eats a piece of flesh from the monster's heart. When the hero discovers that the monster has glided onto dry land, he cuts a large opening in the monster's side and escapes. Freed from his confinement, he is able to liberate others who were devoured and trapped by the monster.

The Night Sea Journey is a profound individuation story. "Individuation" is the term Carl Jung used to describe the process of healing the split in the psyche to become more integrated and balanced. In the opening stage of the individuation process, the unconscious (water monster) swallows you which alters your consciousness and changes you dramatically (being heated and losing hair). Over time and through many struggles, you integrate deeply hidden unconscious contents into consciousness (eating the heart) until the split in the psyche is overcome and you achieve balance and wholeness. This intense experience frees you from the domination of the unconscious. Released from its grip, you attain a new kind of consciousness with freer choices and the ability to help others change.

The Night Sea Journey is not one you have the choice to take. You're pulled into it without warning. Once the journey begins, you have very little control over it. Like a great tidal wave, it carries you along to an unknown destination. During my journey, I recorded hundreds of dreams in order to keep track of changes in my unconscious. The following chapters draw on many of those dreams to reveal how individuation evolves and eventually unites the divided fragments of the psyche into a whole.

At the end of a Night Sea Journey, you live in what Alan Watts called the "wisdom of insecurity,"[2] where the mysteries are honored and you learn to dance without anything under your feet. You live in the moment, straddle the center line within yourself, and embrace doubt as a source of wisdom.

2

Before My Transformation

My deep interest in personal development began in my late thirties when I experienced a mid-life crisis. I questioned the meaning of my life, which led me to look for alternatives to being a professor at the University of Colorado in Boulder where I had been teaching for several years. During that time, I was offering an experiential course entitled "Self and Consciousness," which focused on personal development. Seeing my students evolve in positive ways as a result of our work together, I decided that becoming a Jungian analyst might help me overcome my crisis of meaning. Determined to make a new change in my life, I met with a Jungian analyst in the fall of 1975, which was to become more than six years of intensive and challenging inner work.

Jungian analysis is based largely on dream work so I kept a detailed dream diary from the beginning of my analysis. Dream work penetrates into the depths of the unconscious to eventually bring the conscious and unconscious parts of the psyche into balance. Shadow work is the primary focus of that effort. It includes an in-depth examination of the neglected parts of the psyche which are pushed into the personal unconscious through repression. My first shadow dream fell on the night of November

1976:

    ■ "I'm riding a bicycle down a street when I see someone peering out from behind drapes which have been closed in a basement apartment. I stop and watch. The person draws the drapes open a bit more and I see a man. Then, suddenly, he draws the drapes wide open and standing before me is a mean-looking member of the notorious motorcycle gang, called the Hell's Angels."

At the time, I regarded that Hell's Angel as an image of my repressed negative qualities, including the evil part of me that could kill for the pure pleasure of it. This was the beginning of a pattern of dreams which revealed dangerous men and animals trying to hurt or kill me.

January 1, 1979:

    ■ "I'm with a group of people and we're being chased by a bear inside a building. We become trapped in a room and the bear is trying to knock down the door. I climb up on top of a wall which doesn't reach the ceiling. While I'm sitting there, the bear breaks through with such great force that the door crashes to the floor. At that point, I notice it's not a bear after all, but a tall, burly man dressed in a bear costume who looks very mean and angry."

Images like these were revealing my aggressive instincts. Besides brutish men and dangerous animals trying to kill me, I witnessed images of pure evil, where destruction was its only purpose. Not only did I discover my great potential to do evil things, but my dreams also revealed my hidden capacity to abuse others and to seek power over them. These were sobering images that I had to take seriously if I was going to fully understand and eventually accept the darker side of my personality.

When I started analysis, my personal identity was one-sided because I had failed to fully integrate into awareness what was deeply hidden in my shadow. Living in a society which emphasizes being a good person, I naturally repressed all my bad tendencies. They were pushed into the unconscious to become my personal shadow. What resulted was a one-sided, positive image which was too good. I wore a social mask to convince others that I was an intelligent person with a kind and loving nature. Since my personal image embraced only one half of the opposites, my personal identity became too one-sided and too positive.

Shadow work was a major challenge because I resisted accepting anything at odds with my one-sided persona. As Jung says, "The Shadow is a moral problem that challenges the whole ego-personality, for no one can become conscious of the shadow without considerable moral effort. To become conscious of it involves recognizing the dark aspects of the personality as present and real. This act is the essential condition for any kind of self-knowledge, and it therefore creates more than its share of denial and personal resistance."[3]

Besides dream work, I became aware of how I projected my shadow onto other people. This effort to understand my projections required greater awareness. I had to observe what I feared and found despicable in others and then carefully think about how those attributes could be hidden parts of me. I noticed especially how I projected my desire for power and authority onto a few men. It took some time before I was able to recognize and fully accept those power tendencies as a part of me.

During this phase of my shadow work, I wondered how I would incorporate this new awareness into my identity. Having seen my shadow, how much of it was I supposed to act out? I realized that expressing a part of my shadow might be acceptable if the ethical consequences were not extreme, such as expressing anger more often and more freely. However, I also understood that shadow work did not give me permission to be antisocial and destructive, like a Hell's Angel. It was a serious attempt to develop knowledge of the darker side of the unconscious so that, through awareness, I could bring it under more conscious control. By loosening my shadow's grip on me, I hoped to attain a greater sense of personal freedom. Much later, I learned from Carl Jung that "By understanding the unconscious, we free ourselves from its domination."[4]

Another way I did shadow work was to keep track of my forbidden thoughts, including destructive and bizarre thoughts that were at odds with my positive self-image. I noticed how often I wished someone was dead when that person acted in an aggressive way or made my life miserable. Those forbidden thoughts forced me to question my social identity. If I was such a good person, how could I think such terrible things? Like the other parts of my shadow work, keeping track of my forbidden thoughts helped me to learn more about my shadow and to more fully understand the two sides of my nature.

After several years of deep inner work, I became aware of many of my opposing tendencies and my personal identity slowly expanded to embrace them. Carl Jung regarded this expansion of the personality as an "indispensable condition for individuation."[5] He felt that the individuating person had to embrace the opposites and to live in the tension between them. Living in that tension was considered a necessary step in order to achieve balance and wholeness.

During my years of analysis, I became aware of Jung's thoughts about individuation as a process of becoming a more integrated person. I came to believe that achieving wholeness would develop slowly, more like an evolution than a revolution. Committed to that mission, I sought more personal integration through my dream work and my conscious efforts to expand my identity and self-image. Those efforts produced positive changes. By 1979, I considered quitting therapy because I was happy and I enjoyed my life. It was during this time of contentment that I was suddenly thrust into the depths of the Night Sea Journey.

3

Completely Overwhelmed

Having accepted the idea that individuation was going to be a gradual process, I was shocked by the surprising form it took as a Night Sea Journey. Expecting calm seas, I was completely caught off guard when, on May 11, 1980, a great wave from the unconscious suddenly crashed over me. The wave pushed me into the depths of the night sea where a water monster was waiting to swallow me.

On May 10, 1980, the following dreams indicated an impending change of consciousness.

■ "I'm looking at myself in the mirror and my skull is expanding."

■ "I meet a woman who's carrying art work. I ask her if I can see it and she says it belongs to another woman who rolled up her eyes one day and went blind. I am impressed with her crayon art work, which reveals colorful shapes formed into exquisite and beautiful mandalas."

When I woke up the next morning, a powerful energy in the form of a searing, white heat was coursing through my body, concentrated in my eyes, head, and especially along my spine. It felt like a white laser beam making its way through my body and nervous system. The core of my body was uncomfortably hot. Worried that I might be sick, I checked my temperature with a thermometer. I was surprised to find that my temperature was completely normal.

This intense flood of hot energy caused my consciousness to change in a profound way. I could see the life force radiating from living things, as if a magical energy had been there all along my old eyes couldn't see. It was so captivating that I spent days carefully observing the light of nature coming from the plants and flowers I saw everywhere.

As a result of my altered consciousness and the heat, my breathing changed. It became shallow, to the point where, when walking down the street, I became faint and dizzy. At that point, I realized that I was scarcely breathing and would start breathing more deeply. This corrected the problem for a time, but, when I lost consciousness of my breath again, the problem returned. My pace must have been very slow, for, after seeing me walking one day, a student told me that I was moving in slow motion.

During this time, there was a dramatic increase in my capacity to experience life. What I saw was fascinating and beautiful. What I heard was clearer and more moving. I listened to music with such intense feelings that I cried because of the joy I was feeling and the tragedy I was realizing. How could we live our lives in such ignorance, unable to see and hear the life force?

While I was having some positive experiences from the hot energy altering my consciousness, I was also in a state of panic. I was on the verge of being overwhelmed by the white heat that had broken through from the unconscious. At times, its force was so great that I was afraid I would lose consciousness entirely. Feeling extremely fragile and weak in comparison to the energy's power, I felt like a delicate crystal glass that could be shattered with little effort. During that difficult time, I had dreams of fragile crystal, indicating the extremely vulnerable state that I was in.

This tenuous state became more delicate when I began experiencing the invasion of a dark, evil energy from deep within the unconscious. It charged through me unexpectedly and, when it did, I felt terrified. It was in complete control and I was nearly defenseless against it. When it invaded, I tried to keep a grip on myself for fear that the dark force would shatter me.

These invasions of the dark and demonic energy occurred at intervals for six months. Each time an invasion occurred, I resisted, while also trying to understand what was happening to me. It was unlike anything I had experienced or even read about. I had no point of reference for grasping it, so I felt frightened, lost, and completely alone. I asked the same question over and over, "What is happening to me and why?"

Several years later, I discovered an explanation for the invasion of the demonic energy in Rudolf Otto's *The Idea of the Holy*. There, he describes this terrifying encounter with a dark force as part of a profound spiritual transformation. He explains how one who has a numinous experience may not only feel a deep sense of humility but also great panic in the face of what he called the "mysterium tremendum." Being enveloped by this holy presence may feel like the sweeping in of a gentle tide or "It may burst in sudden eruption up from the depths of the soul with spasms and convulsions, or lead to the strangest excitements, to intoxicated frenzy, to transport, and to ecstasy. It has its wild and demonic forms and can sink to an almost grisly horror and shuddering. It has its crude, barbaric antecedents and early manifestations, and again it may be developed into something beautiful and pure and glorious."[6]

Through those difficult times, I was encouraged by the positive side of the experience, the love I felt, seeing the life force everywhere, and the feeling that I had been launched into a major life-transforming experience. My Jungian analyst was also helpful. While he was unable to understand what was happening to me, he encouraged me to just follow the process. He wisely advised me to stay connected to others and to continue living as normal a life as possible.

Determined to keep my social life intact, I carried out my daily responsibilities at the university as best as I could. I still taught my classes, met with my students, and graded papers, but I retreated into isolation whenever it was possible. Often, I felt exhausted from missing sleep the night before, which was one of the effects of the inner heat. Some days I struggled to maintain my composure in the face of the intense heat coursing through me and the effects of my altered state of consciousness. There were moments when my consciousness diminished to the point where I was living in a fog.

At home, I tried to be a good husband and father. In the evenings, I did my share of the cooking and played with my children after dinner, a special ritual of affection I had always enjoyed. But then darkness would come like a welcome time of sanctuary, when I was alone trying to grasp the deeper meaning of my dreams and to understand the origin and purpose of the white heat.

4

Difficult Challenges

Dramatic transformations of consciousness produce many difficult challenges. In the beginning, the greatest challenge for me was dealing with the intense fear that the unconscious was going to overwhelm and destroy me. A dream during that time offered a clear warning of the danger.

June 1, 1980:

■ "I'm at a lake where the water is turning a muddy color. So I go to the top of a cliff surrounding the lake and throw a piece of blue color into the water. When it hits the surface, the water turns a brilliant blue. Then, I see a slide going down into the water. I'm told that going down the slide is extremely dangerous because once a teenage boy went so far under the water that he almost drowned."

Reflecting on this dream at that time, I recognized the very precarious situation that I was in. I was afraid of being completely overwhelmed by the unconscious and either go insane or die. In response to this warning, I fought hard to strengthen my conscious standpoint by exerting my will. I also used active imagination to steady myself. I would imagine myself being stronger than the unconscious forces which, like water on a rampage, were sweeping me along to an unknown destiny.

Another major challenge I faced was the feeling of being

betrayed. When I was really desperate, I would ask, "Why didn't someone warn me about the difficult ordeal of individuation?" I had heard a few people talk about the process of individuation, but not one of them mentioned the frightening and dark side of the experience. In fact, neither of the Jungian analysts I had worked with had even mentioned the difficulties and dangers of individuation. I felt betrayed by them for having created an illusion about individuation while I was totally shocked by its actual form.

For weeks, I struggled with these feelings of betrayal, knowing that they were an obstacle in my way. In time, I realized that, since my analysts had not experienced the Night Sea Journey, they could not have enlightened me about its powerful and disturbing nature. This realization put an end to my nagging resentment, which made it possible for me to continue my journey.

I shouldn't overstate the difficulties I faced because when I felt the life force as love, saw its numinous quality radiating from living things, and experienced moments of inner peace, I knew that something very rare was happening to me.

A vision on June 2, 1980:

■ "I see a man who's a builder and he says to me, 'It's up', meaning that whatever he was building was up, although the feeling was that only the frame of a new house had been erected. Then, as I lay in bed ready to go back to sleep, I thanked the unconscious for allowing me to have the profound inner experience I was having. Instantly, a vision of a man appeared. He said directly to me as if he were in the room. 'You deserve this', meaning that I deserved the special gift that I was being given."

Receiving positive and affirming messages like this from the unconscious contributed to another problem that became a great challenge for me. It was ego inflation. I felt that I had been chosen for a grand, world-saving mission. I developed fantasies of becoming a spiritual teacher, who could help people change their consciousness.

During the first month of my transformation, I couldn't share my experiences with anyone. How would I explain what was happening to me and would anyone believe me? These questions held me back. Then, on June 8, 1980, I decided to share my experiences and struggles with my wife, Mary.

"I finally told Mary about what has been happening to me. While we talked, it became apparent that I should avoid changing my life in a major way. When one has an experience like this there is a temptation to feel superior and to play the role of a spiritual teacher. By allowing my ego to weaken further, I could easily justify this direction by believing it was my destiny. I have to maintain control over myself and not let the experience overwhelm me. The experience is teaching me about the divine magic in the world and it's giving me the capacity to love and to accept love. It's a freeing experience in many ways. Yet, instead of being inflated, I need to fully integrate my experiences and insights into my life."

Mary was so put off by my ego inflation that she actively

discouraged me from thinking I was so special. If she hadn't been in my life at that time, I might have given in to the temptation by deciding that I had been chosen for a special mission. Along with Mary, there was also a realist in me who mounted stiff resistance to this outlandish idea.

Determined to keep a firm grip on reality, I read Jung's chapter in *Two Essays on Analytical Psychology*, "Phenomena Resulting from the Assimilation of the Unconscious".[7] There, he writes about "psychic inflation" and the negative consequences that arise from it, from going insane to becoming a collective symbol where any chance of achieving individuality is lost. Already frightened about losing control of myself, Jung's thoughts forced me to act. Using active imagination, I told my unconscious that I would resist my fantasies about becoming a world saver. This put a strong check on my ego inflation, but it remained a challenging problem over the next few years.

During the individuation process, ego inflation is one of the greatest temptations. As Jung had said, being swept up in fantasies will either drive you crazy or make you into a collective symbol where individuality is lost. There were many times when I said, "If someone had warned me about the dramatic form that individuation can take, I would never have wanted to become whole." Those were moments of despair when I felt completely lost and alone.

5

Changes

There were many times when I prayed that the white heat, disorientation, and invasions of the demonic energy would stop so I could return to normal consciousness and my old life. That fervent prayer was never answered. A door had opened and then it closed behind me. I couldn't go back. My old life was gone. A new and fundamentally different way of thinking and living was just beginning.

My days were a struggle to maintain a normal life while having such an abnormal experience. My nights were especially tough since sleeping was impossible at times. I slept with my back uncovered because the heat concentrated along my spine was so intense. I woke up most mornings feeling tired, not only from the lack of sleep but from the effects the heat was having on my body. It was wearing me out so much that I felt exhausted and in a daze.

Only my Jungian analyst and my wife, Mary, were aware of what was happening to me. I shared freely with my analyst but very little with Mary because I knew she was unhappy about my changes. She was in the midst of an important transition of her own. In 1980, as I was withdrawing because of the difficult changes I was going through, she was venturing into life changes of her own. In 1978, after years of caring for our young daughters and doing volunteer work, she revived her career interests and returned to scientific research. In June of 1980, she took on a challenging new job at the National Center for Atmospheric Research (NCAR) in Boulder. With new confidence, she was determined to overcome her natural introversion and become more outgoing and sociable. With her becoming more extraverted during a time when I was withdrawing made our relationship more difficult.

Creating art helped me through this lonely and scary time. It was strongly oriented to color and order, often taking the form of mandalas, patterns of order reflecting the nature of the Self (God-image). From the very first days of my change, creating mandalas became a necessity, maybe to compensate for my inner chaos but also to celebrate the emergence of the Self. One sequence of colored drawings showed various faces, each with one beautiful mandala eye and a broad smile.

While I was creating many mandalas as an artist, only a few examples appeared in my dreams at the beginning of my change.

June 10, 1980:

■ "A young girl gives me a gift of a white egg. When I leave, she shows my gift to some women. It's no longer an egg but a handful of very shiny, beautiful coins. They are very old and the unusual thing about them is that, on their backs, are elaborately designed mandalas."

Mandalas appearing in my dreams were a clear sign of a mysterious change taking place within me. This became apparent when I started to have experiences of spontaneous hand and arm movements while I was waking up from sleep in the middle of the night, movements of such a highly symmetrical character, they were mandalas in motion.

Diary, June 24, 1980:

"During a dream, I was doing elaborate movements of my arms and hands in the shape of a mandala. I was told by a voice that the movements I was making were a lost language. I was watching the movements carefully in the dream and then, as I woke up, I could see my hands and arms completing a mandala pattern. They rose up into a wide arc, very slowly and gradually, and then my hands created a small circle at the top. There was a sacred feeling about the movements and the circle affected me deeply, for I felt in awe of its beauty."

Several times in the first year, I made spontaneous arm and hand movements in the form of mandalas while waking from sleep. Those movements were recovering the lost language of the Self (God-image), hidden for ages and now emerging into consciousness.

At night, the heat was intense and during the day I was in an altered state of consciousness. This unusual state produced notable changes. Especially striking was an increase in my level of creativity. My thinking became more spontaneous and playful.

For example, I started to view serious situations as amusing. When I noticed a situation becoming too serious, I wondered how a comedian might view it. This launched me into a more playful attitude about what was happening. As a result, I began to lighten up, let my mind play, and have more fun.

When I started teaching at the university in the fall of 1980, I was surprised to see how much more spontaneously I expressed my ideas and interacted with my students. I was less afraid of making mistakes and more eager to play with ideas and fully involve my students in the creative process. This increasing spontaneity resulted in more creative ideas flowing from me and more dynamic discussions with my students. I became more of a risk-taker, where creativity, not convention, governed how I planned and taught my classes.

In the middle of that summer, I was accepted into the Inter-Regional Society of Jungian Analysts to be trained as an Analyst. At the start of the fall semester, not only was I teaching and working in the counseling center at the university, but I was taking my first course at the Jung Center in Denver as part of my training. This was when I started reading Jungian literature. I read Jung's writings hoping to understand the bizarre experiences I was having. Reading his autobiography[8] led me to think that he had experienced the dramatic form of individuation as an ordeal. However, he failed to write about his experiences in detail so I was unable to find the guidance that I needed. I wanted to know what was happening to me, why it was happening, and what to do.

Diary entry, October 27, 1980:

"This was a difficult night for me. Something powerful from the unconscious flooded my body with energy. I knew I had to stay in control, for the force I was experiencing was great and it brought waves of fear. I felt like fine crystal, so delicate that I could easily be shattered. I have never experienced such a powerful surge of energy from the unconscious, which can only make me feel humble while I tremble in the wake of its awesome power."

This experience was related to a dream I had that night.

■ "I see the petals of a flower and they are alive with intense energy, each petal is radiating bright light and color."

When I woke up from this dream, my body was extremely hot. My hearing was especially keen for I could detect the most subtle sounds within my body. I got up, hoping to keep myself together in the face of the intense energy coursing through me. It was so powerful that I was afraid of losing control and being torn apart. To survive this crisis, I meditated for a long time, trying to quiet my mind and overcome my fear. After meditating for about an hour, the energy and heat finally subsided enough so that I could go back to bed.

I eventually fell asleep and had the following dream:

■ "I look up at the mountains above a town and they

begin breaking up so everyone must run for their lives. To get away, I try to catch a train but fail. Then I come to a trail that separates into two paths. One is a white path and it's been the path of sages. A voice tells me that the paths are arbitrary and either may lead to my death."

In the dream, I decide to take the white path, the path of the sages.

6

Turning Points

From the beginning of my change, water played a key role in my dreams. Usually, the water was flooding over the ground or seeping through the walls of buildings I was in. At the time, I knew that water was a symbol of the unconscious, so I interpreted those dreams as me being inundated by energies from the unconscious, which is exactly what I was experiencing in the form of heat and the invasions of the dark energy. One of those water dreams became a turning point.

November 9, 1980:

■ "I'm working at a resort. I turn on a gigantic iron valve and water pours into the valley. People are washed away by the flood. I'm concerned about whether anyone was hurt or killed, so I look down the valley to survey the situation. To my surprise, I see that the water is being contained behind a newly constructed dam and people are rowing around in boats and they're having a good time."

Unlike my prior water dreams where there was flooding, this dream showed that the water was now held back by a strong, new structure. My unconscious was finally contained so I had more conscious control over my situation. The morning after this dream, I felt less threatened, as if the demonic energy that had been attacking me was being held in check. In fact, after that day, there were no more invasions. For the first time since my transformation began, I felt that I might survive the ordeal and, if I was lucky enough, I might attain a new kind of consciousness.

Up to this point, I had misgivings about the changes that were happening to me against my will. When I felt desperate, I wished that I was normal again, that I could see the world in the old way and even get caught up again in the American way of life. With the disappearance of the demonic energy, my feelings about the experience took a positive turn. The difference was that, while I still experienced an altered state, intense heat, shallow breathing, and felt like a social misfit, I was more thankful.

Mid-December of 1980 marked another turning point. Feeling more in control of myself as a result of the demonic energy's disappearance, I felt freer to share my experience with others. When I first shared my experience with a friend, I was surprised by how spontaneously it happened. My friend asked me how I had been. I remember a smile coming across my face, the kind which can turn into laughter. It was also the kind of smile which says, "Are you really sure you want to know?"

I gave my friend the highlights of my experience. He listened, accepting and believing what I said. He said that, while he couldn't really understand what I was sharing, he believed it was happening and he wanted to know more about my change as it unfolded. This made me feel good, although I felt awkward when we parted, wondering how our relationship would change as a consequence of my sharing such strange experiences.

It was a great blessing to finally share something about myself, for I was accustomed to being open with people I cared about. It had been difficult for me to hold back information about myself because it seemed dishonest.

Within a month, I shared my experience again. It was with a woman I liked and trusted in the Jungian training program. I described to her the powerful energy from the unconscious that had suddenly emerged to overwhelm me, the experiences of heat, demonic energy, and disorientation, and my fears of dying or going mad. I also shared a few positive experiences and changes, plus my hopes and fears.

When I was finished sharing, she said that she had had an experience similar to mine. I became excited. Finally, I had found someone who had gone through the ordeal and could give me guidance! She began to describe experiences she considered unusual in connection to her art. As I listened, I was surprised to discover that her experience wasn't like mine at all. She had simply interpreted my experience in a way she could understand. Her sharing was genuine, so I did not tell her that our experiences were of an entirely different order.

This brief encounter was interesting because I realized the difficulty of communicating an extraordinary experience to someone who has no firsthand knowledge of it. I was also very disappointed. For a few minutes, I thought I had found someone who had had a similar experience, something I desperately needed to help me overcome my loneliness and lack of clear direction. Afterwards, I wondered what it would be like to meet someone who had made the Night Sea Journey and would say to me, "I have experienced the white heat, the terror, and confusion. I know the suffering and loneliness." That person would be able to give me reassurance and information about the course ahead. This was a daydream of hope which revealed how much I needed understanding, support, and guidance. I felt so isolated, afraid, and lonely that I was desperate to meet someone who knew, by direct experience, what I was going through. I was being torn apart and I needed to know how I was going to be put back together. I needed hope that things were going to work out.

7

Ecstasy

Heat, fear, disorientation, desperation, loneliness—these words explain the major part of my experience beginning on May 11, 1980 when I was overwhelmed by unconscious forces that were beyond my understanding and control. But, during this chaotic time, there were extraordinary moments of bliss that lifted me up and gave me a new view of reality.

May 23, 1986:

■ "I see a tree. There is something that looks like a tube which starts at the bottom and makes its way to the top. At the top, the tube is twisting like a snake and a bright white light is emanating from it, blinding to look at."

This dream revealed the intense experience I was having as white light made its way into my brain to create states of ecstasy. Those experiences of bliss were the most beautiful and timeless experiences of my life. They had a profound impact on me, even though they lasted for only a short time. These rare experiences of ecstasy were spread across four years. There were 4 occurrences in 1983, 3 in 1984, 3 in 1985, and 2 in 1986. After 1986, the blissful experiences stopped. Often, these moments of ecstasy occurred while I was wakening up from dreams in the middle of the night, although they also happened during the day.

Diary entry, October 22, 1983:

"I was in my study lying on the couch when energy filled the lower part of my body then it began to move up my spine until it reached my head. At that point, I fell into a state of complete bliss and peace. For a few seconds I was in rapture."

These experiences are impossible to describe. It was as if I had entered a type of reality which was really true, while my sense of normal reality was fiction. There was a feeling that I had entered a higher spiritual reality, beyond time and space, and it was what people experience when they pass into the afterlife. A dream captured the essence of this feeling the following year.

November 7, 1985:

■ "I'm preparing to make a big transition of my internal state. I begin to feel myself change as a feeling of ecstasy begins to overwhelm me to the point where I begin to cry uncontrollably from relief and joy. Then I reach a state I can't describe for my mind has no context for grasping it. But, when I entered that state, all motion ceased, as if everything were frozen in a single moment of time."

Everything frozen in a single moment of time expressed the feeling I had several times of entering eternity. But it was more than eternity. It was something so beautiful I can't even describe it. The perfection of God is the closest I can come to capturing how I felt at the time. I wondered, "Was it possible for such a reality to exist independently of our everyday sense of the truth, hidden from our awareness?"

Sometimes the white energy rose slowly, which made the

experience of bliss gentle. On November 1, 1983, I was meeting with a graduate student to discuss his dissertation. As I was listening to him explain his work, a strange sensation began to develop at the back of my neck. In a few seconds, energy began to rise up slowly from my neck into my head. As it moved up, I entered a blissful state, accompanied by feelings of peace and freedom. The feelings of bliss rose and fell in harmony with the surges of energy. The experience lasted about twenty minutes and it altered my consciousness for the rest of the day. While teaching that afternoon, I was surprised by the spontaneous and playful way I taught my class.

At other times, the surge of energy was powerful, causing me to fall into a more profound state of ecstasy.

Diary entry, March 29, 1986:

"As I woke up from sleep, I could feel a charge of heat running up into the lower half of my skull. It took the shape of a bubble, expanding outward until it filled a large space. As the shape grew larger it became brilliant white, then the bubble burst, sending the energy outward, fragments of light traveling at a great speed. At that point, I heard myself cry out, 'Oh, my God, my God', for I fell into a state of ecstasy which filled my whole being. I lay in bed for some time afterwards experiencing the afterglow of this spiritual experience, which took no more than a few seconds."

When I experienced ecstasy, I felt as if I were inside a bubble of joy and contentment, nested in God's perfection and love. These were some of the most beautiful and meaningful experiences of my life and I will never forget them.

8

Learning about Kundalini

In the fall of 1980, I quit doing psychological counseling at the university with students and I withdrew from the Jungian training program. I also stopped going to my weekly Jungian therapy sessions, feeling that they were becoming more of an obstacle than a help.

During that time, I was inundated by the heat, inflated, confused, and lonely, but I was also happy, playful, and creative. Then, during February 1981, there was a sudden breakthrough when I learned about kundalini. While going through a profound change, one needs an interpretation to understand it. What I learned about the rise of kundalini energy and its dramatic impact on consciousness gave me that understanding.

Dream diary, February 14, 1981:

"I made a startling and wonderful discovery--that the rising of kundalini produces the experience I'm having. At the bookstore, I accidentally came across Gopi Krishna's book, *Kundalini: The Evolutionary Energy in Man.* I read small portions of it with intense fascination. I returned from the bookstore with that book and two others which seemed helpful. I was so happy, I can't describe it. Finally, I'd found a point of reference for my experience other than Jung's. Also, there were ideas about what to do in Gopi Krishna's book and from two other books I purchased, *The Ultimate Transformation* by Dr. R.P. Kaushik and Lee Sannella's, *Kundalini: Psychosis or Transcendence?* That night I was very excited to explore my experience more fully, and I felt hopeful that my process would eventually unfold in a positive way."

I can't express strongly enough the significance of finding a body of literature that described the experience I was having, including my moments of ecstasy. Up to that time, I felt lost and without a point of reference for understanding my changes. Beginning to read about kundalini put my experience into a broader, historical context. Finally, I had a way to understand what I'd been going through.

In the following days, I read everything I could about kundalini. I wasn't interested in reading theoretical treatments of the subject, which make up the bulk of the literature, because they failed to describe the kundalini experiences I was so eager to learn about. Only rarely did I find works which seemed to be backed by experience. I read those books carefully, especially Gopi Krishna's account of his transformation. Although his experience was more powerful and threatening than mine, the similarities were striking.

While meditating in 1937, Gopi Krishna's kundalini was awakened. "Suddenly, with a roar like that of a waterfall, I felt a stream of liquid light entering my brain through the spinal cord."[9] This liquid light was the mystical heat which racked his body and mind to the point where he was afraid he might die or go mad. "Little did I realize that from that day onwards I was never to be my old normal self again, that I had unwittingly and without preparation . . . roused to activity the most wonderful and stern power in man, that I had stepped unknowingly upon the key to the most guarded secret of the ancients, and that thenceforth for a long time I had to live suspended by a thread, swinging between life on the one hand and death on the other, between sanity and insanity, between light and darkness, and between heaven and earth."[10] When I read statements like this, I knew I had found a kindred spirit. Here was a man whose experience could inform and guide me, and I could definitely understand his suffering.

He described the days after his painful initiation as a "prolonged nightmare," when he became gripped "by a feeling of horror of the supernatural."[11] Faced with these many disturbing developments, he lost interest in work and conversation. He was caught up in great confusion and fear about what was happening to him. "I passed every minute of the time in a state of acute anxiety and tension, at a loss to know what had happened to me and why my system was functioning in such an entirely abnormal manner. I felt exhausted and spent."[12]

Deeply troubled by his condition and feeling fragile to the point of breaking, he was unable to share his experience with anyone. "No one could even suspect what was happening to me inside. I knew that but a thin line now separated me from lunacy, and yet I gave no indication of my condition to anyone."[13] He was afraid that others wouldn't accept the truth of his account, given its bizarre nature. This drove him into isolation, although his wife was a great source of comfort and support.

In time, the intensity of the white energy became warm and pleasing rather than hot and burning. Yet, he was still afraid, disoriented, and longed for guidance. "From the very first day I felt myself walking on a ground that was not only unfamiliar but presented such queer formations that, losing my bearings and self-confidence, I trod hesitatingly with utmost caution, fearing a pitfall at every step. I looked around desperately for guidance, only to face disappointment on all sides."[14]

His meditations were part of a spiritual practice whose cultural underpinnings pointed to the goal of enlightenment. Yet, what he had been told about the nature of enlightenment was a far cry from his profound and overwhelming kundalini experience. This disparity made him feel betrayed.

Gopi Krishna's ordeal lasted for many years, although the most frightening occurrences of energy and heat appeared at the beginning. After suffering a great deal over that time, he came to see the experience in a positive light, as the rare transformation of consciousness attained by the ancient ones.

> "In the primary stages, . . . the vital current appeared to be acting erratically and blindly like the swollen water of a flooded stream which, pouring out through a breach in the embankment, rushes madly here and there trying to scour out a new

channel for its passage. Years later I had an inkling of what had actually happened and could guess at the marvel lying hidden in the human body, . . . when, ploughing its way through the flesh like the diverted stream in flood, it creates new channels in the nervous system and the brain to endow the fortunate individual with unbelievable mental and spiritual powers."[15]

Reading Gopi Krishna's account frightened me because I could see that some kundalini experiences end in disaster, but it also gave me hope because I realized that the process had a definite form, evolved in a certain way, and, in the end, it could produce positive changes. Finally, I had a way of understanding my experiences. This was a great blessing during a time of great need!

9

Encountering a Guru

I was struck by a comment Gopi Krishna made about the necessity of having a guru when someone is overwhelmed by kundalini energy. This started me wondering where I could find a spiritual teacher to give me guidance and support. While I was in this receptive mood, a guru from a local religious community came to see me. He was with his wife and a follower, who was a neighbor of mine. The guru was about 30 years old. He had long blond hair, was dressed in white from top to bottom, and he carried a long, white staff. He told me that he had heard from a graduate student of mine that I was studying kundalini. He had come to see me to learn about my interest in kundalini. I felt that this was an odd but meaningful coincidence because I'd just begun to think that I needed a guru. I needed a teacher who had experienced the awakening of kundalini and could guide me along the path that I'd been forced by nature to take.

When the guru, his wife, and my neighbor were seated in my front room, the guru asked me to explain why I was interested in kundalini. Before I could say anything, the guru's wife spoke up. "I'll bet he's studying kundalini because he wants to experience it." I laughed to myself as I thought about what I'd been through. I wondered if I should I tell them about it. At that

43

moment, I felt a lot of ambivalence toward them. I hoped that they had had a direct experience of kundalini so they could give me some advice. However, I was very suspicious of her blank expression as she tried hard to look enlightened and by his white clothing, long blond hair, long white staff, and knowing smile. There was something phony about both of them.

Even with these ambivalent feelings, I decided to share my experience. I described what I had been going through in the briefest terms, while they laughed after each dramatic incident. It was the kind of laughter that conveyed firsthand knowledge of the heat, the fear of madness and death, the demonic attacks, the loneliness, and disorientation. Yet, I was ambivalent. Was their laughter based on real knowledge or was it just a performance?

Then something strange happened--I became extremely cold. At first, I felt chills and then they turned into disturbing tremors. I covered myself with a blanket that was draped over the couch, which must have seemed odd because the temperature in the room was warm. I hoped they wouldn't notice my tremors. When the shaking got worse, I drew the blanket up to my neck, trying to stop the shaking and to calm myself. They talked and I shook. It was strange. Luckily, they finished what they wanted to say and got up to leave.

When they were standing on my front porch, the young guru promised to call me. Still shaking from the intense chills, I went to my study to meditate. My thoughts kept returning to what had happened. Were my tremors a reaction to a spiritual energy in the guru? Was he the guru I needed? That night I had a dream about a refrigerator with a fire inside. This made me wonder whether the cold tremors I had experienced were related to the inner heat that was racking my body. Later, I learned that having cold chills and tremors are common experiences after a kundalini awakening.

Up to this point, I had avoided encouraging the process of change in any way. I meditated for the necessity and pleasure of it, not to speed up the process. However, when I learned from my reading that kundalini goes through stages, I began to create "spiritual ambition," the desire to stimulate change through the use of definite practices. For the next two months, meditation became a tool, not just a pleasure. I meditated hoping to trigger a deeper spiritual experience that would heal me.

On Friday, April 10th, I received the promised telephone call from the guru. He invited me to his house to hear some poetry, verse which spoke of the ultimate transformation, or union with God. I welcomed the opportunity, for I still wondered whether he was for real and further back in my mind was the idea that he might become my guru. He greeted me at the door with a knowing smile and then a warm hug.

I was escorted into the living room, decorated as one might expect. There was a large, hand-carved chair set aside for him and a number of impressive wall hangings. The room had a sacred feeling, but it was formal rather than comfortable and relaxed. Soon his wife joined us, followed by a disciple who poured tea and then left quietly after performing her role with grace and obedience.

Pausing only long enough to get my bearings, I asked the guru and his wife to tell me about their kundalini experiences. Both of them hesitated, as if they were looking for something to say. This puzzled me for I knew that anyone who experienced the power of kundalini could never forget it. The possibility that they were withholding the experience didn't seem reasonable, because they labored to share something, however general and off the mark it was. As I suspected from our first meeting, the wife was living out the idea of the change without having experienced it. Underneath her blank expression, she seemed tense and afraid. I didn't trust her.

When the young guru spoke, his words came in broad generalizations about experiences he had had. He used the jargon of kundalini but without giving specific evidence that he had experienced its power. Without that experience, his account came across as false and unbelievable. I wanted to ask, "How can you pretend to have had a kundalini experience and not say one word about the burning, terror, and disorientation?" For an instant, I wanted to be direct and shake the truth from them. Catching myself, I pulled back.

I decided that the young man was trapped in his guru image, so I chose to watch and listen to the interesting drama he was performing. After listening for a few minutes, I began to feel intensely hot all over, especially in my head. In a few more seconds, my consciousness changed drastically. My mind became so quiet that I had to call forth my words with effort, like trying to awaken children from their naps.

When I left the guru's home, my body felt like it was suspended in fire. Arriving home, I went directly to my study, where I began to meditate. I asked my unconscious for help because I was feeling desperate physically. While meditating my head was alive with intense vibrations, as if the top of my skull was lifting off and back. Then, I saw a dream image of Robert Redford, the film star, which became interchangeable with an image of the young guru. I took this to be a message from the unconscious that the young guru was only a good actor after all. Realizing this guru couldn't help me, I decided not to see him again. I realized I would have to go on alone, without the help of a teacher. This was a sad moment for me.

10

Early Signs of Healing

The first year of my transformation was a combination of heaven and hell, but, as the year drew to a close, there were positive signs of change. New healing themes emerged in my dreams. Androgyny surfaced for the first time and, in a dream, my skin shed like a snake's during its yearly renewal. Although there were moments of crisis when the hot energy from the unconscious tested me, these new themes were signs of healing which gave me comfort and hope.

Beginning in April of 1981, the conventional view of masculinity--characterized by power and aggressiveness--was being modified within me as my feminine and masculine tendencies forged an androgynous alliance. This androgynous state becomes a reality when the opposites, characterized as female and male, merge to produce greater wholeness. This sense of inner harmony appeared in my dreams as the genders taking on each other's attributes.

April 8, 1981:

■ "I'm sitting in a café when my sister and two nephews show up. My nephews are wearing women's high heeled shoes. One is wearing a skirt, a very feminine blouse, make-up, and his hair is fashioned like a woman's. As we are walking together, I ask them why they're dressed like women. They say they're starting a new women's fashion line for men."

May 22, 1981:

■ "I see a young woman wrestling playfully with her children. I sense that it must take a toll on her. Then I notice that the woman has a fairly well developed dark mustache. She runs her finger across it and I can see the hairs are very fine like they are in the mustache of a sixteen-year-old boy."

I was happy to see the appearance of androgyny in these dreams. It was a sign that important changes were continuing at an unconscious level without my active participation. It amazed me to discover that individuation has a life and logic of its own, with its own stages of growth and forward momentum. My consciousness was being reconstructed by healing forces deep in the unconscious. Those forces were changing me. I remember saying to myself, "What a miracle!"

In the beginning of May, I had a dream that warned me of an impending and dangerous change. That change began in the middle of the night on May 15, 1981. When I woke up, my body felt unusual and my eyes seemed slightly crossed. As I sat in meditation, my spine became extremely hot, so much so that it was uncomfortable leaning back on my pillow. My whole body was hot, although the heat was concentrated along my spine. I sat on the floor in order to avoid leaning back against anything. It was extremely uncomfortable sitting without back support but cooler. While meditating, dream images and auditory sounds (people saying strange things to me, cracking sounds, like bones breaking) occurred one after the other. Perhaps a second or two separated them from each other.

I awoke from the dream about 2:30 a.m. and by 4:00 a.m. the dream-like visions and sounds were still occurring in rapid order. I returned to bed wanting to get some sleep but my body was so alive with energy, vibrating so dramatically, I couldn't sleep. Instead, the dream-like visions and sounds continued until 6:00 a.m. At that time, I had a vision which was more vivid and longer than the others. I see a human back and the skin is an orange color. As I look at it, my eyesight becomes microscopic so I can see the fine details of the skin's surface. I notice small blisters all over it. Then, I fell asleep and had a dream.

■ "I take my shirt off, look in a mirror, and see that my back is peeling from a severe burn. It's not just one layer of skin but several layers that have been burnt. I begin pulling off huge sheets of loose skin. Underneath, I can clearly see a new layer of healthy skin."

When I woke up from this dream, I began thinking about snakes shedding their skin as a sign of renewal. This dream also reflected the intense heat I was experiencing in my body that night, suggesting that the heat was part of an initiation ritual which would eventually produce a new life.

For the next several days my spinal column was hot up to the point between my shoulder blades. The intense heat was concentrated there in a large ball, as if it were being blocked from rising upward. This forced the energy to radiate outward into a full circle. It was very hot which made me feel uncomfortable. Full of fear, I waited for what might happen next.

During the following week, the heat concentrated between my shoulder blades began pushing its way into my lungs, which made them burn. On May 22, 1981, this led to a frightening experience.

Diary entry:

"I woke up about 5:00 a.m. breathing very heavily. My breathing was irregular, alternating between shallow and deeper breaths. It felt as if the mechanism which normally controlled my breathing had stopped for I found myself having to force myself to breathe. I got up from bed and sat in meditation. My breathing remained irregular. I was in a state of panic because I felt that my breathing could stop at any moment. I concentrated on controlling the fear while I tried to steady the rhythm of my breathing. The heat in my lungs, which had begun to develop a few days before, was intense. In fact, my whole chest was filled with heat. Surprisingly, my heart was very quiet. As I sat in meditation, there were moments when my breathing and heart rate became so weak, I was afraid they would stop. At that point, I would have to breathe deeply to compensate for the shallow breathing. I thought about going back to bed but I was afraid my breathing might stop entirely if I didn't control its rhythm. Finally, after sitting for over an hour, my breathing became more regular and I began to feel more comfortable. Eventually, I was able to return to my bed, exhausted from the experience but relieved."

The next day, my breathing remained labored until noon.

The heat was concentrated in my chest and lungs, but the heat in my head and the persistent burning sensation in my eyes were far less intense, so physically I felt more comfortable. Although the experience had been frightening, I wanted to believe that this dramatic movement of unconscious energies would contribute to my healing.

Then, in a dream on November 7, 1981, I was told how I would evolve. A voice said that I would become "wings without a body." At that point, I was shown a pair of wings flying without a body. This movement conveyed the idea that my consciousness would reach a point where it would exist on an even keel, without wild fluctuations of mood or emotion. In fact, at years end, I was experiencing states of inner peace.

Diary entry, December 17, 1981:

"Something new has begun. Quite often now I enter a deeply peaceful and completely fulfilled state. This has been noticeable since the beginning of December. During these experiences I feel free from inner conflict, like something is fitting together so perfectly in my psyche there is complete harmony."

These peaceful states occurred more frequently and were of longer duration as time passed. This was the beginning of what I called entering the "Nest of God," a feeling of living in the center of the mandala, which is the Self's exquisite and completely balanced state.

11

Transforming the Darkness

The first year of my change was the most challenging experience of my life. Thinking back to that time more than thirty years later, I can still remember the intense feelings of fear and loneliness. It was a very scary, disorienting, and exhausting time. During the first two years, I experienced the heat night and day, which wore me out. After the second year, the heat occurred regularly but intermittently until about 1987 when, reaching the end of my journey, the heat stopped. Throughout that time, I recorded my dreams in great detail every night. By observing my dreams, I could see my unconscious slowly changing. As it changed, I changed.

From the beginning of my dream work in 1975, I was frequently chased by aggressive men and dangerous animals. During the seven years of my Night Sea Journey, I watched as men gradually quit attacking me and dangerous animals lost their killer instincts. From late 1982 to March, 1988, I had twenty-seven dreams which showed dangerous animals in a docile state, including lions, bears, dogs, and a great white shark.

October 26, 1986:

■ "I'm walking up a mountain after a beautiful, white snow has fallen. I step on a bear that has been covered by snow.

I'm concerned that it might attack me, but it's sleepy and cold, so its aggressive nature has disappeared."

January 5, 1987:

■ "I'm with a man and woman who are my guides. With their help, I'm going to be interacting with a very dangerous creature. The guides take me into a deep ocean pool, where I encounter a great white shark. To my surprise, it's playful and friendly. I can swim alongside it and pet it at will. Then the scene changes and I'm waiting in line to get into a building. Only certain people can gain entrance to it and a woman is the guardian of the gate. She asks me for some sign that I'm qualified to enter. I show her my arm and there are scratches on it from the teeth of the shark. These were put there by accident when the shark was playing with me. This is the sign that I can enter the building, for the woman realizes that I am now on very friendly terms with all of life's devouring creatures."

When I first began to work with my dreams, I was afraid of the unconscious. Nightmares of being chased by dangerous men and animals contributed to that fear and, during the first part of my transformation, I was terrified by its dark and uncanny power. By 1987, I no longer feared it. Instead, I was in awe of its healing power.

In the early years of my therapy, toilets in my dreams were dirty, clogged, and full of feces and urine and bathrooms were filthy. Toward the end of my change, they were clean and white.

June 9, 1986:

■ "I'm standing in a large open-air shower basin which is

also a toilet. Apparently, the idea is that both the inner and outer parts of the body can be cleaned. I get down on my hands and knees and begin scrubbing the shower basin with a bleach cleanser to remove the dirt which turns it completely white."

By the end of 1986, there was no filth in the toilets or bathrooms. The following dream shows the cleaning work was finished.

December 17, 1986:

■ "A cousin has come to visit me and he tells me that he really likes my bathroom because it's so clean and white."

Paralleling the themes of aggressive animals being tamed and toilets and bathrooms being cleaned were dreams of ugly creatures and dark substances being removed from my body.

August 20, 1985:

■ "My wife and I are participating in a healing workshop. I'm pulled aside by a doctor who begins to examine my right eye. He takes a cotton swab, dips it into a chemical solution, and begins to wipe my eye out. To our mutual amazement, he pulls out a terrible-looking creature, quite large and with pincher arms. I notice a couple of grubs that have also been extracted. I realize that my eye will now function as it was intended. I am relieved to know that my eye has been healed."

In this dream, it is the right eye that is healed. In a later dream, the left eye has a defect. It, too, is eventually healed so both of my eyes can see clearly. As a result of this cleaning, I felt freer from the aggressive instincts and negative emotions that had disturbed and distorted my thinking. No longer at the mercy of those drives and emotions, I felt more stable and balanced. I was beginning to live as I had been promised–as "wings without a body." It dawned on me that being balanced and whole is how human consciousness is meant to be.

October 25, 1988:

■ "As I'm walking through a neighborhood, I notice that someone is remodeling the basement floor of a house. They are putting in very large windows in order to let in more light."

This dream made me aware of the change I had been experiencing. The large windows in the basement apartment symbolize a fundamental change between the conscious and unconscious parts of my mind. The light of consciousness can now penetrate the darkness of the unconscious to reduce its negative influence. This is the meaning of the dreams I had about seeing clearly. Consciousness was beginning to play a much larger role in my life and disturbing thoughts and negative emotions were losing their power over me. This positive change would eventually give me much more control over my thoughts and emotions.

As I came closer to the end of my Night Sea Journey, I realized that the dreams of aggressive animals being tamed, cleaning, and things turning pure white were parallel images of a purification process taking place within me. Thirty-eight dreams dealing with white or something being cleaned to the point of whiteness occurred between the years 1985 and 1987.

February 26, 1985:

■ "I see a round, white plate. There are a few small pieces of dirt or food stuck to it. I take my finger and begin cleaning them off. Soon, the plate will be completely white."

March 1, 1986:

■ "I'm holding a carton of cottage cheese in my hand. The carton is totally white for there's no writing on it. I open the lid and the carton is filled with white cottage cheese. The whiteness of everything is emphasized. Then, I suddenly notice a defect where a small piece of the white carton is missing."

Diary entry, March 1, 1986:

"I'm beginning to see connections between the dream image of the defective cottage cheese container and other dreams that I've had lately, for example, a green lawn with a small dry spot, the absence of a small amount of water in a water bed, and food without quite enough salt. All these images have been communicating the same thing, that my purification process isn't complete."

Several dreams of white, or nearly white, objects occurred during the month of March, 1986. Although it wasn't clear why the images were alternating between being completely white and nearly white, there was a gradual evolution toward purity. While this change was moving slowly, it was encouraging to see my unconscious changing and to experience its effect on me.

Diary entry, March 7, 1986:

"Something beautiful is happening to my consciousness as the day goes on. I feel that I'm standing inside an immense bubble where I'm so alive with positive energy that tears come to my eyes out of joy. I'm feeling close to the end."

Afterwards, I experienced two more dreams about whitening and both revealed objects in a pure, white state. In one dream, I see some dog excrement and I'm surprised by its color, which is pure white. In a culminating dream, gold appears as a symbol of resolution.

October 14, 1987:

■ "I see three white dogs, a mother and her two puppies. The puppies come to me in a very playful mood. The biggest one rolls over on its back so I'll scratch its stomach. I'm surprised to discover that its belly is the color of pure gold."

The gold color on the puppy's stomach felt like a sign of completion, for gold is a well-known symbol of wholeness.

12

Emerging Balance and Wholeness

On August 6, 1985, I was told by a voice while wakening up from a dream that there's a part of the psyche whose purpose is to harmonize the opposites in order to create a balanced state of wholeness. As I watched my dreams slowly evolve, I witnessed this coming together of the two sides of my nature. In my dreams, the opposites first became distinctly separated until they achieved the equality of identical twins. Then the identical twins merged to create a new third element that was balanced and whole. When this unification was finally achieved, the "Philosopher's Stone" appeared--a state where flexibility and stability are combined to create a new way of being.

Between the years 1984 and 1986, my dreams revealed the opposites becoming untangled and then reaching equality.

May 4, 1984:

■ "There's a tough man who is running roughshod over people. I see a man hit him as hard as he can in the chest yet the bully doesn't flinch. But when I begin fighting with him, I can easily throw him around. I'm thinking of killing him but I can't for I clearly recognize that there is a perfect balance of good and evil in him."

September 26, 1984:

■ "I see two trees of equal size intertwined with each

other in the form of a spiral. Neither of the trees have leaves but both are very much alive. In fact, where the trees are intertwined, there is an immense amount of powerful energy."

Two identical trees intertwined, with energy at their point of union, confirmed what the voice from the unconscious had told me. There is a part of the psyche whose sole purpose is to heal the split in the psyche. When this healing is achieved, peace and freedom are close at hand, as the following dream reveals.

December 1, 1984:

■ "I see a choir singing on the street. It's composed of about an equal number of black and white people. As the two groups sing together, I notice how beautifully they sing. Then, the idea is conveyed to me that I am becoming quiet, like a church."

I noted this change in my dream diary on December 1, 1984:

"The dream of the choir connects to a new phase for me. I feel as if a huge conflict has ended in me, which is producing something like the peace and quiet of an empty church. Not only inner peace but a deep feeling of happiness and creativity, so hard to describe, is growing within me."

In Jungian thought, what is known as the "Quaternity" is the perfect balance of four equal parts, which is a symbol of the Self (God- image) and a sign of wholeness. In the last few years of my transformation, the Quaternity was revealed in my dreams.

October 25, 1985.

■ My home address is shown as 2222 instead of its actual number.

October 16, 1987:

■ "I'm in a garage which is submerged in the ocean. A flat, square boat is there. I'm told that it was built for the ocean. There are three other people with me and each of us sits on a corner of the square boat which stabilizes it in the water. The boat moves out of the garage and out to sea. I see another group of people trying to balance their boat, but their boat doesn't have four corners, so it won't stay in balance."

What an interesting image! Only when four people are sitting in the four corners of the square boat will it become stable. At a personal level, this integration will give a person the ability to remain balanced even in rough times.

On June 2, 1986, I was told by a woman in a dream, "What remains is that the two become one." This was a turning point, as the opposites began to merge to create a greater sense of balance within me.

April 28, 1985:

■ "I find an old cloak with a bottle inside. Inside the bottle are some old trinkets, but one in particular is quite a find. It's an old amulet which has two gold wings attached to a circle. It is shaped like a mandala and it feels magical and sacred. It has been hidden for many years and has now been found."

January 24, 1986:

■ "I'm at the foot of a large mountain which has been in

the process of reconstruction for several years. It had been taken down and a new skeletal structure was added, then earth was replaced to cover it. I see a section where the bones of the skeletal structure are showing and I notice that the joints come together there. Pins have been placed at the joints so it's possible for the parts to move. This means that the mountain can move, for flexibility has been built into its structure. I'm amazed by this achievement."

July 1, 1986:

■ "A man hands me a ball made of a flexible material, like the children's play dough called 'silly putty'. I know it's the Philosopher's Stone. When I take the stone in my hand, energy flows into me which gives me the gift of flexibility."

The mountain with a moving skeleton and the ball of silly putty are images of the Philosopher's Stone, which combines solidity and flexibility to create the unity of the Self.[16] With greater balance, I felt more stable and calm. Having greater flexibility, my creativity flourished.

These were changes that happened to me, not changes I worked to create on my own. That is the miraculous nature of individuation when it takes the dramatic form of a Night Sea Journey. Once the unconscious swallows you up, it begins to transform you. My dreams show how those changes happened and how, as the deeper part of the unconscious changed, my consciousness also changed. These were not superficial and temporary changes, but deep and long-lasting ones. It was like being torn apart by the unconscious and then put back together in a new way. It definitely felt like a death and rebirth experience.

After seven years of severe trials and healing, I had arrived at the point of the Night Sea Journey when I could cut my way out of the water monster's belly. Through unconscious changes that I could never have imagined, I had become balanced, happy, and creative. With the Philosopher's Stone in my hand, I was ready to leave my isolation and return to society.

13

My Return

By 1987, I felt like a different person. Feeling reborn, I wondered what calling to pursue in society. I could turn to art and writing to cultivate my creativity. I could also seek reentry into the Jungian Training Program and, if accepted, go on to become an analyst and help others through the individuation process. For several months, I pondered what direction to take while I carried on my normal life as a teacher, husband, and father. Then, as fate sometimes dictates, I was drafted to lead my department at my university. After several years of isolation, I was thrust into the challenges of leadership. This was to be an interesting test of my new consciousness.

While leading my department, I discovered that I could respond to challenges with balance and flexibility in mind. I could embrace and respond to circumstances as they arose, for I had come to the Taoist position of living in the moment and adapting to life. Following the rhythm of each moment, I no longer thought much about the past and I focused on the future only when planning was necessary. I lived more fully in the moment and developed a lighthearted orientation toward the many problems I faced every day.

Since I felt less attached to the social world, I had fewer

personal goals for shaping my department. I was free to follow whatever direction my colleagues wanted to take. My approach disturbed those who urged me to develop a stronger leadership style with more definite goals. In response, I told them I was taking them on a walk through the forest and, while there was no clear path, we were heading somewhere. That was a Poohish thing to say. Like Winnie the Pooh, our meandering through the forest did lead us somewhere and without the conflict that arises when there are definite goals to fight about.

I was in harmony with John Heider's balanced point of view in *The Tao of Leadership*, where he says, "The wise leader runs the group without fighting to have things a certain way. The leader's touch is light. The leader neither defends nor attacks."[17]

It became very clear to me that my new consciousness was in harmony with Taoism, for I was living according to the First Principle of the Tao that anything taken to an extreme will produce its own correction. Lao-tzu comments on this principle:

> If you hope to be expanded, first contract.
> If you hope to become strong,
> you should first weaken yourself.
> If your ambition is to be exalted,
> humiliation will follow.
> If you hold fast to something,
> it will surely be taken away from you.

<blockquote>This is the operation of the subtle law
of the universe.[18]</blockquote>

Wholeness is not perfection, but treading this middle path, where all aspects of the personal psyche are redeemed and lived. This is what I call the "self-forgiving path," for much is allowed and little condemned. In the years prior to my change, I applied a standard to myself that undermined my well-being, for I had to be too good, too smart, and too nice. After my change, I was freer to express my dual nature. I could be smart or stupid, engaged or detached, and playful or serious. Jung discussed individuation in terms of this expansion of personality which unites the opposites, making for a new and better way to live.

By the end of 1987, I had more control over my thinking. I knew that I was not my thoughts, they were not necessarily true, and I had the ability to manage them rather than be under their control. For example, when I was grappling with problems while leading my department, I would catch myself in the thought, "This is a tough problem." I would pause to reflect, realize that thought was just a point of view and that I could change it to a new thought, like "This is a challenging problem." The thought that the problem was tough made me want to avoid it; whereas, by thinking that the problem was challenging, I felt inspired to solve it. Once I understood that my thoughts were simply ways of perceiving reality, I could choose to change them. Using this approach, I gained more control over my thinking, which made me more effective as a leader.

Being more stable and also more flexible, my creativity flourished. The creative spirit made its way directly into my art, leadership, and teaching. By cultivating a more creative life, I realized Benjamin Hoff was right when he said, "When you discard arrogance, complexity, and a few other things that get in the way, sooner or later you will discover that simple, childlike, and mysterious secret known to those of the Uncarved Block: Life is fun."[19]   After my change, I was more playful so I was having more fun leading, teaching, and socializing.

Not only was I having more fun, but I felt supported by a strong foundation so my consciousness remained steady and positive. About this change, Jolanda Jacobi says, "The conscious possession of the Self can give a man a feeling of lasting security through the relation he has found to the God-image."[20]

14

Kundalini and Alchemy

Kundalini and alchemy are ways of understanding the dynamics of individuation as a Night Sea Journey. These ideas are explored for those who want to learn more about the forces that shape individuation as an ordeal and a healing process. Advice is also offered for those who are in the midst of this personal crisis.

Being engulfed by powerful energies from deep in the unconscious, fears are likely to arise, including the possibilities of a serious illness, impending death, or insanity. During this frightening time, it is wise to set fears aside and follow the process patiently, accepting the fact that it may last for several years. Positive interpretations of the experience may also come to mind, such as thinking it is the opening phase of enlightenment.

The temptation may be strong to completely withdraw from the social world. This urge should be resisted, for it is important to maintain a strong conscious standpoint to survive the heat and the frightening experiences that appear without warning from the unconscious. By staying anchored in rational thinking and social commitments, consciousness is strengthened, which increases the individuating person's ability to respond to the crisis.

Personal transformation is a mystery, since its underlying causes cannot be fully understood. For this reason, it has been given different names and described in various ways from culture to culture. In some cultures, it's called "kundalini," when the energy, depicted as the goddess Shakti, is released at the base of the spine and then travels upward, breaking through a series of seven chakras, until she is united with her masculine counterpart, the god Shiva, at the crown chakra.

While I was in the midst of my crisis, reading books about kundalini energy helped me understand my experience and gave me assurances that what was happening to me had a form that could lead eventually to a positive outcome. By reading Lee Sannella's description of the many manifestations of kundalini awakening, I learned that many of my physical symptoms--heat and cold, abnormal breathing, arm and hand movements, visions, and sounds--were part of the kundalini process. I discovered that my feeling of detachment, the slowing down of my thoughts so thinking took conscious effort, and my ego-inflation were the results of kundalini energy being released.[21] Most reassuring of all was Gopi Krishna's account of his kundalini experiences because it gave me an understanding of the bizarre experiences I was having.

Reading about kundalini made me long for a guru, since many books on the subject strongly recommend having a teacher.

There are many who would agree with Yogi Amrit Desai when he says, "The guru's grace is essential on this path."[22] Especially in the initial stages when confusion is the greatest, this statement rings true, since sound guidance is desperately needed at that time. For the initiated who will have experiences beyond normal consciousness and without assurances of the outcome, finding a guru may be a big help, if one can be found who has experienced the rising of kundalini and can give practical advice. However, it is also important to realize that the Night Sea Journey has its own evolutionary momentum, purpose, and outcome. During the early stages, it won't seem like it, but, at the end looking back, the elegance of the process is revealed, as if an invisible hand had been guiding it from the start.

During 1989, I learned about an even more compelling explanation than kundalini to understand my experience. It was Carl Jung's use of the alchemical process as an avenue for understanding individuation. I was surprised to discover that my experiences fit into the alchemical stages of transformation that Jung and others had described, especially Marie-Louise von Franz and Edward F. Edinger. I was surprised because I had assumed that alchemy was simply a metaphor for understanding individuation, not a description of the actual process. When I saw how alchemy could help me understand my unusual experiences, I undertook a serious study of it.

I learned that alchemy has existed for hundreds of years in numerous cultures around the world. It was thought to have a chemical foundation, based on the belief that certain laboratory procedures had the capacity to transform base metals into gold, which symbolized spiritual perfection and the attainment of eternal youth. Chemical experiments were undertaken whose brews were consumed with the hope of living forever, but most of them led to a violent illness or death. Although it seems absurd when viewed as a literal chemical process, alchemy offers a useful symbolic representation of psychological processes that lead to wholeness.

Jung resurrected alchemy for psychology when, puzzled by the strange dream images of some of his patients, he turned to alchemical symbolism for understanding and insight. There, he discovered hidden psychological meanings within its chemical procedures. Alchemists were seeking to create the Philosopher's Stone, which was a symbol of personal healing and wholeness. Yet, this effort was risky. Jung says, while "the alchemical opus is dangerous," it creates positive outcomes when "the human soul is completely integrated."[23]

The danger was due, in part, to the heat and terror which accompanied the process. One alchemical text says that the only way purification of matter can begin is "by means of the inward heat of the body."[24] This inward heat was widely associated with

God and, according to Edinger, represented archetypal energies which transcended the personal ego and were experienced as powerful and numinous (spiritual).[25]

The common thread between kundalini and alchemy is the union of opposites. With kundalini, Shakti and Shiva merge at the crown chakra to create a state of oneness. With alchemy, the Philosopher's Stone emerges when the opposites are separated and then reunited. We may not understand what creates these forms of personal transformation, which we call "individuation," but it seems clear that they both produce a unification of the personality that "rectifies all one-sidedness."

The alchemical process has three broad stages, depicted as colors: Black (nigredo), white (albedo), and red (rubedo). The point of the work is to purify the filth in the personal psyche by constant heating and washing. During the whitening phase, the opposites are separated, so the union of the male and female can take place. When that androgynous state is reached, described by alchemists as the "chymical marriage," the adept has entered the next stage of the process.

There are specific procedures within these three broad stages. Edinger, in separate issues of *Quadrant*, discussed them at length. They are briefly summarized here.

The first procedure is "calcinatio." During this difficult operation, heat is applied to the dark substance within the psyche to turn it white. Edinger says the final result of the heat is the creation of white ash, which corresponds to the notion of "white foliated earth" in alchemical texts and is called the whitening phase of the procedure.[26]

"Solutio" is the second procedure. Whereas heat is the purifying agent during the first stage, water works on matter during this second procedure to turn it into its originally undifferentiated state of wholeness. Edinger says that "Bath, shower, sprinkling, swimming, immersion" are common dream images during this procedure. "All of these images relate to the symbolism of baptism which signified a cleansing, rejuvenating immersion in an energy . . . transcending the ego, a veritable death and rebirth."[27]

"Coagulatio" is the third procedure. After very careful washing separates the opposites, this procedure reunites them to create something heavy and permanent. Edinger says that this is the joining of the ego with the Self, the symbol of wholeness.[28]

"Sublimatio" is the fourth procedure and, like the other procedures, it is connected to the purification process. The coagulated substance of the preceding operation is subjected to more intense heat, which causes it to break down into a white powder and become vapor.

The fifth procedure, called "mortificatio," refers to killing and is associated with "putrefactio," which is the process of decay. Edinger says, "Mortificatio is the most negative operation in alchemy. It has to do with darkness, defeat, torture, mutilation, and rotting." [29] However, these dark images often lead to highly positive outcomes, including resurrection and rebirth.

The hallmark of mortificatio is the color black. What is rotten and decayed is ultimately whitened, as fire and water work on the filth to purify it. What dies is the evil in the psyche, which may be what we call "original sin" today. When this occurs, the devil is no longer thought to be an autonomous force in the unconscious since it has come under the control of the conscious part of the psyche.

During the sixth purification procedure, "separatio," the cleaning continues, with the added step that the opposites are separated and made equal. This twin state is preparation for their final union. Edinger puts it this way, "The two protagonists: sun and moon, husband and wife, earth and spirit, stand for all the pairs of opposites. They must be cleansed from contamination with each other...." When their complete separation is achieved, the purified opposites can be reconciled in the "coniunctio," which is the crowning goal of the alchemical opus. [30]

"Coniunctio" is the final procedure of the work, when the opposites merge to produce the sense of wholeness characterized as the Philosopher's Stone. The stone emerges, Edinger notes, "by a final union of the purified opposites and, because it combines the opposites, it mitigates and rectifies all one-sidedness."[31]

For most people, individuation is likely to develop as the result of an evolutionary process, but my experience shows that it can also be an ordeal, a more terrifying and traumatic path to wholeness than is commonly believed in Jungian circles.

15

Individuation and Alchemy

Individuation lies at the very heart of Jungian thought and practice, for the main goal of depth analysis is the psychological regeneration of the individual. Many people leave analysis after resolving pressing psychological issues, but there are others who continue, often confronting the deeper layers of the unconscious. According to Murray Stein, there are two phases of analysis. The first phase is gaining insight into issues that exist in the personal unconscious and the second is encountering archetypal material from the collective unconscious. He says that the "success of analysis as a whole depends upon the first of these phases being largely accomplished before the second is entered."[32]

This preparation period is important because the person in analysis must have a strong enough ego to successfully assimilate the powerful energies from the collective unconscious. Jolanda Jacobi argues that confronting these "primordial images" is dangerous because the archetypal motifs are supercharged with powerful numinosity (energies). In her view, individuation is analogous to the "quest of the hero" which requires "a strong and resilient ego, and also, if all the dangers are to be overcome, the constant surveillance of a skilled and perceptive therapist with a stable personality...."[33]

During my transformation process, it was impossible to say anything intelligent about the form it took. Only in retrospect does a coherent picture appear. Examining the seven years of my change, there is overwhelming evidence to support Carl Jung's view that individuation is alchemical in nature. The heat and moments of terror, the evolution of my dreams, and the stages of my transformation were in close alignment with the alchemical procedures. Alchemists knew that the heat released in the body was a necessary part of the purification process, for the heat was responsible for burning away the filth in the psyche and for bringing the opposites together in unity.

Cleaning with water was also an alchemical procedure for eliminating filth. This washing is said to occur over and over again, some say nine times, some fifteen times, and others say for ten years. In short, it's a long process, but through constant washing the dark matter eventually turns white.[34]

In her book about the nature of alchemy, von Franz explores the transformation of St. Thomas of Aquinas. At one point in his writings, he spoke about the Holy Ghost as a kind of chemical agency which heats, cleans, and purifies. During my transformation, a voice told me that my change was being forged by the "Holy Spirit" working within me as "hot ocean."

Hot ocean, the elemental fire, was the cleaning agent working on the filth in my psyche to turn it white. Since the ocean is regarded as a symbol for the collective unconscious, the notion of "hot ocean" implies that the energy I was experiencing was coming from a deep layer of the unconscious. Jung says that by descending into the unconscious, the conscious mind puts itself in a perilous position, for it is apparently extinguishing itself.[35] This flooding of the conscious mind by the unconscious has disturbing consequences. Not only does it diminish the concreteness of consciousness, which makes you feel that you are disappearing, but it alters consciousness, so you feel reborn.

Changes in my behavior were further indications of this rebirth; the abrupt change from being extraverted to being introverted, the increasing control I had over my thoughts and emotions, and the sudden appearance of lighthearted fun and spontaneity. These are different manifestations of the alchemical process. As von Franz says, the individual is likely to become quieter and more detached during the whitening process. About the appearance of spontaneity, she says, "The alchemical stage of reanimating the body . . . corresponds to the psychological goal of 'conscious spontaneity', i.e., participating in the flow of life consciously yet without analyzing everything."[36]

Aggressive figures, clogged toilets, and dirty bathrooms in my dreams symbolized the filth the alchemists repeatedly washed until it became white. This dark stage, von Franz notes, is often the first stage of the work.[37] When dark aggressors appeared in my dreams, I worked with them as part of my shadow, exploring and acknowledging my aggressiveness and my potential for doing evil things. However, the dreams of clogged toilets and dirty bathrooms really baffled me. At that time, I was unaware that they symbolized the filth within me that would eventually be purified. Edinger says, "Feces, excrement, and bad odors refer to the putrefactio. The common dreams of neglected or overflowing toilets which plague puritan-minded people belong to this symbolism."[38]

Cleaning is an act of separation. Black matter is being separated from the white and the opposites are being untangled so they can unite. When the opposites have attained this equality, their union is said to be near.[39] When separation and equality is achieved, the whitening stage is over and the red stage (the union of opposites) begins. At this time, "'all colours' appear, as if the peacock were spreading his shimmering fan."[40]

In alchemy, the appearance and harmonizing of the colors is an indication that the work is coming to an end. In my case, this resolution was revealed in separate dreams where many colors appear on the surface of a completely clean porcelain toilet, a child's bed is inlaid with "mother of pearl" reflecting its many colors, a couch has multiple colors blended together in perfect harmony, and colored snakes are laid side by side to create a beautiful rainbow effect. The rainbow integrates the colors, which the alchemists regarded as a sign that God was coming.[41] The rainbow was regarded as a symbolic forerunner of the Self and an indication of approaching unity. Jung says that the many colors are mentioned in alchemical texts to indicate "something like totality." During the red stage of the work, the colors unite which "for many alchemists was the climax of the work." At this point, the "original state of disunity" is overcome and "the unified man" is created.[42]

For the alchemists, the goal of personal transformation was the "miraculous entity" they called the Philosopher's Stone. Its creation could only come about when the opposites had been completely purified and then recombined to correct all one-sidedness. The alchemists regarded the stone as a watery solid, balancing solidity and flexibility in a state of wholeness.

As von Franz says, the Philosopher's Stone is a "great paradox" since liquid and the most solid thing were regarded by many alchemists as the same thing. When the stone emerges, "something firm is born, beyond the ups and downs of life" and something living is born "which takes part in the flow of life."[43]

Once the Philosopher's Stone forms, everything becomes internally "quiet and still," for the resolution of inner conflicts has been achieved. Von Franz captures the nature of this change:

> If through fighting and meeting the unconscious
> one has suffered long enough, a kind of objective
> personality is established; a nucleus forms in the

person which is at peace, quiet even in the midst of the greatest life storms, intensely alive but without action and without participation in the conflict. That peace of mind often comes to people when they have suffered long enough: one day something has been born which remains in the centre, outside or beyond the conflict, which does not go on any more as it did.[44]

Von Franz goes on to say that the person who gives birth to the stone, which is "flexible but unshakable," is "no longer easily dissociated and swept away by emotion."[45] At that point, "The state of helplessness in which one is caught by one's own inner processes stops, which amounts to a tremendous steadying of the innermost core of the personality; that is comparable to the Philosopher's Stone, which is symbolically what the steady inner experience forms."[46] This new kind of consciousness makes the suffering, loneliness, and disorientation of the Night Sea Journey worth enduring.

Having dreams of completely white objects, pure water, and the many colors of the rainbow, the unconscious signs were clear that my "psychic disunity" was ending by 1986 and the opposites were merging within me. This change was reflected in dreams of twin objects separating and then fusing together, of four identical objects in balance, and of a transcending third element arising from the opposites. In alchemy, the formula for this change is called the Axiom of Maria, "One becomes two,

two becomes three, and out of the Third comes the One as the Fourth."[47]

What was separated during the "fiery" conflict unites to create wholeness. According to Jung, the opposites naturally "flee from each other," but they also strive for balance, for sustained conflict within the psyche is at odds with life. Having become worn out from the process of being separated, they eventually succumb and are drawn together into the sacred bath where they dissolve into one another.[48] When the separated opposites unite, the psyche shifts its focus from the ego to a new center (the Self) so it naturally stays in balance, symbolized in my dreams as a white staff that stands upright on its own and a top that will spin forever.

16

Individuation as a "Spiritual Emergency"

Christina and Stanislav Grof have devoted their lives to a careful study of individuals who have experienced a profound personal transformation and they are the founders of a caring network which provides counseling services for them. Their published works--*Spiritual Emergency*[49] and *The Stormy Search for the Self*[50]--are important for understanding transformations of consciousness and the various ways that individuals handle such sweeping changes. Like Jung, they understand these changes to be part of the evolutionary potential of human beings, leading to wholeness. Their view is that "Spiritual development is an innate evolutionary capacity of all human beings. It is a movement toward wholeness, the discovery of one's true potential. And it is as common and as natural as birth, physical growth, and death-- an integral part of our existence."[51]

Many of my experiences were similar to those described by the Grofs, since they draw heavily on the testimony of people who have been on a Night Sea Journey. I am one of many who have experienced what they call a "spiritual emergency," a term they use to imply spiritual emergence with the added element of crisis. They say, "Spiritual emergencies can be defined as critical and experientially difficult stages of a profound psychological

87

transformation that involves one's entire being. They take the form of nonordinary states of consciousness and involve intense emotions, visions, and other sensory changes . . . as well as various physical manifestations."[52]

It is quite common for people who experience a spiritual emergency to report fears of dying or going insane, and some report dramatic experiences of energy flooding into their bodies.

> People can feel consumed by strange and at times overpowering bursts of energy. They might feel pulsing electrical charges, uncontrollable tremors, or sensations of some unknown force streaming throughout their systems. Their heart rate may increase and their body temperature rise. Why does this happen? These manifestations are often a natural physiological accompaniment to abrupt changes in consciousness; they may also be specific characteristics of a certain form of spiritual emergency, such as the awakening of Kundalini.[53]

The Grofs have also described various responses to the assimilation of these powerful energies from the unconscious. From the cases they studied, they found that some people:

> Recoil from the prospect of having to reshape their identities,
>
> Mistrust the new reality they have entered,
>
> Are overwhelmed by the thought they might go mad,
>
> Feel unworthy of the experience as if they don't deserve

it,

> May only experience transcendence temporarily and feel depressed when they compare it to the mundane aspects of normal life,

> Hang on to the higher experiences and resist any tendency toward normalizing their lives, and

> Develop ego-inflation and messianic tendencies which, if expressed, alienate them from others.[54]

In my experience, a person may have several of these reactions at different times in the process.

Looking back, I realize how difficult it is for family members and friends who must adapt to the changes in the individuating person. Recently, while listening to my wife talk about the tough time she had dealing with my change, I felt more sympathy toward her, knowing how hard it must have been to live with me during that time. In their chapter, "Guidelines for Family and Friends," the Grofs say: "Living with someone who is going through a spiritual emergency is often very demanding for everyone involved. Those close to that person, as well as the person himself or herself, spend much time and energy on the changes that are being brought into their lives, and friends and family are regularly confronted with their own emotions and limitations. Seemingly normal and stable relationships become threatened by abrupt shifts in one person's interests and behavior that often require an unwelcome adjustment on the part of others."[55]

This is especially true in the beginning, when the changes are powerful and the individuating person is caught up in crisis and ego-inflation. As greater wholeness is achieved, the benefits of the struggle emerge, so even a spouse, who has shared in the suffering, may end up liking the outcome. As my wife admitted, "You turned out well."

The positive changes I experienced seem usual for people who have made the Night Sea Journey, for the Grofs discovered similar changes among the people they studied. Many felt:

> More appreciative of life in general and more centered in the present moment.

> Less driven to prove something to the world and happier with whatever is available to them.

> More attracted to simple, uncomplicated aspects of their lives, more prone to cultivate quiet and peaceful pursuits, and more able to enjoy solitude.

> More appreciative of other human beings and more likely to enjoy contact with them.

> Less concerned about social approval, how they present themselves, and whether they are successful.

> More contented, more positive about themselves, and more sensitive to the world around them.

> More creative, drawn to writing, painting, dancing, singing, or new creative outlets within their careers.

More self-accepting, more tolerant of others, and
more appreciative of differences.

More unified and connected with everything and
everyone around them.

Less self-centered and more likely to redirect their focus
to include others.

More special and full of grace, but also more
likely to see others as equally unique and blessed.

More in need of living honestly.

More loving and compassionate for themselves, others,
and the world.

More connected to an inner source, higher self, or God.

More appreciative of everything in the world around them
as an exquisite display of God's handiwork.

More in harmony with life, knowing resistance causes
unnecessary pain.

More aware of the importance of spirituality in
their lives and their need to develop it.[56]

There is no doubt that the Night Sea Journey is an ordeal;
yet, as these results show, the outcomes are largely positive. For
example, in contrast to my past way of being, I'm now more
balanced; more spontaneous, creative, and playful; more able to
live in the moment without resistance; more able to keep things
in proper perspective; more accepting of others; more grateful for
natural and cultural diversity; and more appreciative of life. I am

also less at the mercy of my thoughts and the social pressures of society, less concerned about what others think of me, and less afraid of death.

Among all of my changes, the most remarkable is the steadiness of my new consciousness. As the voice from within my unconscious predicted, I have become "wings without a body," so I'm no longer cast about by wild fluctuations of mood or easily swept away by negative emotions.

17

Managing My Mind

In my new state of consciousness, I began to notice that I had better control of my thoughts and could shape them. This led to the realization that I could change my thoughts in ways that would make me happier and more contented. As a result, I began to create thinking practices I've been using ever since and have found they are helpful to others. This is not easy work. It requires diligence and persistence in the face of setbacks. Here are some of the practices I use.

Put it into perspective

Many people suffer from making their problems bigger than they actually are. Some people might inflate the size of their problems to add drama to their lives while others might want to feel like martyrs. When the size of a problem I'm facing seems big, I think to myself, "Put it into perspective." Then I ask myself "How big will this problem be tomorrow, in a week, a month, a year, or my lifetime?" Often, this simple question reduces the size of my problem, which increases my ability to deal with it in a constructive way. Reducing the size of my problems by putting them into the perspective of time has improved my ability to solve problems rather be overwhelmed by them.

Don't take it personally

Getting upset by other people's words or treatment is quite common. I can ruin a perfectly good day by fuming about it. I might feel hurt, because I've taken it to heart. To stop this downward emotional spiral, I think to myself, "Don't take it personally." It might be my problem, so I need to think about that, but it might be the other person's problem. "Don't take it personally" makes me more aware so I can clearly evaluate the situation and make a conscious choice about it. By reducing the number of times that I take things personally, I have reduced the number of my emotional upsets. This has not only improved my relationships, but it has helped me maintain my inner balance, which has given me more peace of mind.

Don't take it too seriously

This is a thinking practice I use a lot while I'm playing tennis. I've learned that, when I'm taking a point, game, or match too seriously, I lose my inner balance. Being too serious, I make too many errors, which frustrates me to the point where the game isn't fun. Also, when I'm in a conversation with someone, if I start taking it too seriously, I can quit listening and start pushing my ideas too hard. The reminder, "Don't take it too seriously" keeps me in balance, so both my tennis and life work better. Are there issues I need to take seriously? Of course there are, but there are also many issues that I don't need to take seriously.

Stop the putdowns

When I was younger, I tried to cover up my inferiority by creating a positive self- image as a confident and friendly person. Even though I became popular in school, there were times when I put myself down and suffered the negative consequences. After my change, when I could see the damage that the putdown game creates, I quit playing the game. By using the thinking practice, "Stop the putdowns," I reduced the number of times I criticized myself and other people. When I did, my life and relationships improved in a hurry.

Practice kindness

Kindness is one of the important keys to a happy life. The beauty of kindness is that it can be used in two ways. We can be kind to ourselves by treating ourselves well and we can extend kindness to others through understanding and compassion. To make kindness an important thinking practice, I've created what I call "The Wheel of Harmony." It goes like this:

Be kind.

Can't be kind?

Then try appreciation.

Can't show appreciation?

Then try acceptance.

Can't accept?

Then try kindness again.

Keep trying until the wheel of harmony
makes a beautiful sound.

When I can't feel kindness or appreciation for certain people, accepting them, with all their shortcomings, helps me to reach the point where kindness and appreciation toward them become possible.

Try to forgive

When I accepted my personal weaknesses as part of my wholeness, I quit being so hard on myself. This has made it easier to forgive myself when I make mistakes, have selfish feelings, and have dark and forbidden thoughts. Being able to forgive myself for those things, I've learned to more easily forgive others when their dark side emerges or when they behave badly. Being able to forgive keeps me from getting stuck in self-accusations and criticisms of others. At times, when I can't forgive myself after hurting someone's feelings, I ask for forgiveness. It helps clean up the relationship so I don't have to dwell in the past and can be more fully in the present.

Quit resisting what you can't change

This is the thinking practice I use most often. When I'm frustrated about something in my life, I ask myself "What am I resisting that I can't change?" It might be something simple, like the long line in front of me at a grocery store checkout counter, red traffic lights when I'm late for an appointment, or just getting older. When I realize that I can't change what I'm resisting, it becomes obvious to me that continuing to resist will be futile and a waste of time. So, I stop resisting. When my resistance stops, I recover my peace of mind.

Who am I to judge?

We automatically judge others and ourselves in light of our beliefs, social norms, and social expectations. When someone falls short, we criticize and belittle them, sometimes in our minds and at other times to their faces. When someone hits the mark, we think positive thoughts about them. When we fall short, we condemn ourselves, which can lead to a depression. When we hit the mark, we feel good about ourselves, which elevates our self-esteem.

When I catch myself making a negative judgment of another person, I can put a stop to it if I remember the thinking practice, "Who Am I to judge?" This simple practice makes me conscious of my judgment, so I can stand back from it and make a conscious choice. I might decide that the judgment is justified, but I might also notice how arbitrary and hurtful it is to the person I'm judging. When I give up my judgment, I offer acceptance. Judgment tends to close down the mind while acceptance keeps it open. Judgment can hurt; acceptance can heal.

It could be worse

When I've had a bad day, I can start feeling sorry for myself. If I catch myself sinking into that "poor me" state of mind, I think to myself, "It could be worse." As soon as I say this to myself, I start thinking of other circumstances that could be far worse. Acknowledging those comparisons wakes me up to the fact that things aren't that bad and, in fact, other people have far bigger problems than I do. This simple shift of thinking from self-pity to "things aren't that bad" opens the way for me to pursue new possibilities. With less darkness and more light in my thinking, I'm able to deal more effectively with life's challenges.

Request a change

Complaints are a normal part of relationships, yet, when we receive a complaint, how do we react? Do we respond with understanding or resistance? Let's face it; we don't like receiving complaints. It annoys us and even makes us angry at times. So, is there an alternative to complaining when we want someone to make a change? Yes, instead of lodging a complaint, we can request a change.

When I'm on the verge of lodging a complaint, I take a moment to remember the thinking practice, "Request a change." This simple thought moves me away from the complaint to something more likely to produce a good result, which is "I have a request to make." Then I try to make that request without anger or blaming. It doesn't mean I will get my way in the matter, but it increases the likelihood that I will.

Put a stop to envy

Envy is a fire which burns in our hearts and minds. When it gets out of control, it can become deadly, ruining our feelings for others and tarnishing our self-esteem. Envy boils down to three thoughts. "I want what you have. I dislike you for having it. In comparison, I also dislike what I have." The fire of envy can't rage in me without comparison. Someone else has to have in abundance what I want. My thinking practice, "no need to envy" helps me to bypass envy so I can be thankful for the life that I have.

Feel life wealthy

We think of wealth in terms of money, but money is only one form of wealth. If we can breathe, if we can laugh, if we can walk, if we can look up at night into our universe with all its beautiful galaxies, stars, and planets, if we are loved and love others, if we have shelter and something to eat--that is all part of our wealth. Money is important, but become aware of the many other forms of wealth that we possess. When I start feeling down on my luck, I stop and think to myself, "Hey, I'm life wealthy!" This thought wakes me up to the fact that, while my life isn't perfect, I am life rich!

Fear is a big exaggeration

Fear is a common human emotion and it causes more than its share of suffering. Yet, if we think carefully about our fears, we will realize that most, if not all, are big exaggerations. If we were to go through our lives from 10 years old to our current age, how many of our fears would have come true? I would guess that our fears come true about one to five percent of the time. We tend to exaggerate the size of our fears as a survival tactic, in order to remain safe and to avoid injury and embarrassment.

I definitely have my share of fears, which are especially ominous during the night. When I'm experiencing a fear, I ask myself, "What is the realistic probability that this fear will come true?" Usually, I come up with a one percent chance. As soon as I see that my fear is an exaggeration, I'm more willing to do what my fear wanted me to avoid.

I get to

How often on any given day do we say to ourselves, "I have to?" For example, "I have to go to a meeting," "I have to write a report," "I have to cook tonight" or "I have to take out the garbage." I learned the thinking practice "I get to" from my good friend, Bill. One day, I told him that I had to go home to do some gardening. He said, "What about thinking that you get to do some gardening?" "What do you mean?" I asked. His response: "When you think you have to do some gardening, it feels like a burden that you'll want to avoid. When you think 'I get to' do some gardening, it feels like a privilege that you're lucky to have." I realized in that moment that I was lucky to be healthy enough to work in my garden, which made me think about all the people who, for physical reasons, weren't as lucky as I was. When I catch myself in the thought "I have to" I shift to "I get to" and what a nice difference it makes in my attitude!

I'm good enough

Every day we go on a roller coaster ride as our moods swing up and then take a dive. What's creating this roller coaster existence? Our ego-size is constantly expanding and contracting, depending on compliments and criticisms, successes and failures, good news and bad news. When a situation causes our egos to deflate, we may feel sad or fall into a depression. I find that I can stop these ego deflations by reminding myself that, while I'm not perfect, "I'm good enough!" When circumstances in my life make me self-critical, this thinking practice keeps me from going into an ego tail spin. It's like a net that catches me in freefall so I can recover my balance, make a conscious choice, and restore my ego's size to "just right," which is not too big and not too little.

****

These are thinking practices I use to navigate the many challenges of my life. Changing thinking patterns isn't easy. It requires practice and persistence. A friend of mine told me how a tennis coach taught his players to elevate their effectiveness on the court. He said,, "It will take 20,000 repetitions to break an old habit until you fully integrate a new ability. Then, it will be a part of you and you will not have to think about it anymore. You'll just do it." The idea of 20,000 repetitions may have been an exaggeration, but he was making a good point. In terms of human behavior, it's fairly clear that our natural tendency is to respond automatically to situations by using our old thinking patterns. Knowing this, we have to assume that it will take many tries before new thinking patterns become a part of us. But, without trying, nothing changes. So, let's keep trying.

Personal Growth Books by the Author

<u>Screwing Up Love or How to Make Love Grow and Last</u> (Createspace, 2013).

<u>Today, I Will . . .Words to Inspire Positive Life Changes</u> (Blue Mountains Arts, 2009).

<u>Why am I so DAMN Unhappy? And What to Do About It</u> (Robert Reed Publishers, 2008).

<u>Blooming: Teachings of a Woo Master</u> (Green Dragon Books, 2005).

<u>The Woo Way: A New Way of Living and Being</u> (Green Dragon Books, 2003).

<u>Playful Mind: Bringing Creativity to Life</u> (Green Dragon Books, 2003).

<u>Awakening Minds: The Power of Creativity in Teaching</u> (Green Dragon Books, 2003).

Notes

[1] Carl G. Jung, "Symbols of the Mother and Rebirth," *Symbols of Transformation*, Volume 5. (Princeton, New Jersey: Princeton University Press, 1956), p. 110.

[2] Alan W. Watts, *Wisdom of Insecurity*. (New York: Random House, 1968).

[3] Carl G. Jung, "The Shadow," *Aion*, Volume 9, II. (Princeton, New Jersey: Princeton University Press, 1959), p. 8.

[4] Carl G. Jung, *Commentary to Secret of the Golden Flower*. (New York: Harcourt, Brace and World, Inc., 1962), p. 122.

[5] Carl G. Jung, "The Structure of the Unconscious," *Two Essays on Analytical Psychology*, Volume 7. (Princeton, New Jersey: Princeton University Press, 1966), p. 297.

[6] Rudolf Otto, *The Idea of the Holy*. (London: Oxford University Press, 1979), pp. 12-13.

[7] Carl G. Jung, "Phenomena Resulting from the Assimilation of the Unconscious," *Two Essays on Analytical Psychology*, Volume 7. (Princeton, New Jersey: Princeton University Press, 1966), pp. 139-155.

[8] Carl G. Jung, *Memories, Dreams, Reflections*. (New York: Random House, 1963).

[9] Gopi Krishna, *Kundalini: The Evolutionary Energy in Man*. (Boulder: Shambhala Publications, Inc., 1971), p. 12.

[10] *Ibid..*, p. 17.

[11] *Ibid..*, p. 49.

[12] *Ibid..*, p. 51.

[13] *Ibid..*, p. 55.

[14] *Ibid..*, p. 91.

[15] *Ibid..*, pp. 118-119.

[16] Jung says the mountain is one of the most common inorganic symbols of the Self. Carl G. Jung, "The Structure and Dynamics of the Self," *Aion*, Volume 9,II. (Princeton, New Jersey: Princeton University Press, 1959), p. 226.

[17] John Heider, *The Tao of Leadership*. (Toronto: Bantam Books, 1986), p. 59.

[18] Ni, Hua-Ching, *The Complete Works of Lao Tzu*. (Malibu, California: The Shrine of the Eternal Breath of Tao, 1979), pp. 28-29.

[19] Benjamin Hoff, *The Tao of Pooh*. (New York: Penguin Books), p. 20.

[20] Jolande Jacobi, *The Way of Individuation*. (New York: New American Library, 1967), p. 75.

[21] Lee Sannella, *Kundalini: Psychosis and Transcendence*. (San Francisco: H. S. Dakin Company, 1978).

[22] Yogi Amrit Desai, "Kundalini Yoga Through Shaktipat," in John White (ed.), *Kundalini, Evolution, and Enlightenment* (New York: Anchor Press, 1979), p. 70.

[23] Carl G. Jung, quoted in Edward F. Edinger, "Psychotherapy and Alchemy, VI. Mortificatio," *Quadrant*, Volume 14 (Spring, 1981), p. 23.

[24] Edward F. Edinger, "Psychotherapy and Alchemy I. Introduction II. Calcinatio," *Quadrant*, Volume 11 (Summer, 1978), p. 36.

[25] *Ibid.*, p. 29.

[26] *Ibid.*, p. 34.

[27] Edward F. Edinger, "Psychotherapy and Alchemy III. "Solutio," *Quadrant*, Volume 11 (Winter, 1978), p. 70

[28] Edward F. Edinger, "Psychotherapy and Alchemy IV. Coagulatio," *Quadrant*, Volume 12 (Summer, 1979), p. 28.

[29] Edward F. Edinger, "Psychotherapy and Alchemy VI. Mortificatio," *Quadrant*, Volume 14 (Spring, 1981), p. 25.

[30] Edward F. Edinger, "Psychotherapy and Alchemy VII. Separatio," *Quadrant*, Volume 14 (Fall, 1981), p. 60.

[31] Edward F. Edinger, "Psychotherapy and Alchemy VIII. Coniunctio," *Quadrant*, Volume 15 (Spring, 1982), p. 10.

[32] Murray Stein, "The Aims and Goal of Jungian Analysis," in Murray Stein, ed., *Jungian Analysis*. (Boulder: Shambhala Publications, Inc., 1982), pp. 36-37.

[33] Jolande Jacobi, *The Way of Individuation*. (New York: New American Library, 1967), pp. 46-47.

[34] Marie-Louise von Franz, *Alchemy, op.cit.*, p. 220.

[35] Carl G. Jung, "The Prima Materia," *Psychology and Alchemy*, Volume 12. (Princeton, New Jersey: Princeton University Press, 1968), p. 325.

[36] Marie-Louise von Franz, Alchemy: An Introduction to the Symbolism and Psychology. (Toronto: Inner City Books, 1980, p. 333.

[37] *Ibid.*, p. 208.

[38] Edward F. Edinger, "Psychotherapy and Alchemy VI. Mortificatio," *Quadrant*, Volume 14 (Spring, 1981), p. 29.

[39] *Ibid.*, pp. 221-222.

[40] Carl G. Jung, "The Paradoxa," Myterium Coniunctionis, Volume 14. (Princeton University Press, 1970), pp. 75-76.

[41] Edward F. Edinger, "Psychology and Alchemy VI. "Mortificatio," *Quadrant,* Volume 14 (Spring, 1981), p.29.

[42] Carl G. Jung, "Rex and Regina," *Mysterium Coniunctionis*, Volume 14. (Princeton, New Jersey: Princeton University Press, 1970), p. 285.

[43] *Ibid.*, p. 174.

[44] *Ibid.*, p. 169.

[45] *Ibid.*, p. 264.

[46] *Ibid.*, pp. 237-238.

[47] *Ibid.*, p. 288.

[48] *Ibid.*, pp. 285-286.

[49] Christina Grof and Stanislav Grof (eds.), *Spiritual Emergency: When Personal Transformation Becomes a Crisis.* (Los Angeles: Jeremy P. Tarcher, Inc., 1991).

[50] Christina Grof and Stanislav Grof, *The Stormy Search for the Self.* (Los Angeles: Jeremy P. Tarcher, Inc., 1991).

[51] *Ibid.*, p. 1.

[52] *Ibid.*, p. 31.

[53] *Ibid.*, p. 51.

[54] *Ibid.*, pp. 69-72.

[55] *Ibid.*, p. 169.

[56] *Ibid.*, pp. 229-232.